SPACE

Steve Parker

Copper Beech Books
Brookfield, Connecticut

CONTENTS

4   What if the telescope hadn't been invented?

6   What if space weren't space?

8   What if a space probe tried to land on Saturn?

10   What if we had many moons?

12   What if comets didn't return?

14   What if the Sun went out?

16   What if there were no stars at night?

18   What if the Universe started to shrink?

20   What if there were no spacecraft?

22   What if rockets hadn't been invented?

24   What if the spacesuit hadn't been invented?

26   What if we could travel at the speed of light?

28   What if there were Martians?

30   Factfile and glossary

32   Index

Designed and produced by
Aladdin Books Ltd
28 Percy Street,
London W1P 0LD

First published in the United States
in 1995 by
Copper Beech Books, an imprint of
The Millbrook Press
2 Old New Milford Road
Brookfield, Connecticut 06804

Library of Congress Cataloging-in-
Publication Data

Space / by Steve Parker : illustrated by
Peter Wilks. p. cm. -- (What if...)
Includes index. Summary: An
imaginative look at space with such
questions as "What if the Sun went
out?" and "What if there were
Martians?"
ISBN 1-56294-912-8 (lib. bdg.) --
ISBN 1-56294-947-0 (pbk.)
1. Outer space--Miscellanea--Juvenile
literature. [1. Outer space--
Miscellanea. 2. Questions and
Answers.] I. Wilks, Peter. ill. II. Title.
III. Series: Parker, Steve. What if--
QB500.22.P37 1995 95-23980--
500.5--dc20 CIP AC

Editor
Jon Richards

Designed by
David West Children's Books
Designers
Rob Shone, Flick Killerby
Illustrator
Peter Wilks – Simon Girling and
Associates
Printed in Belgium

WHAT IF THERE WERE NO INTRODUCTION?

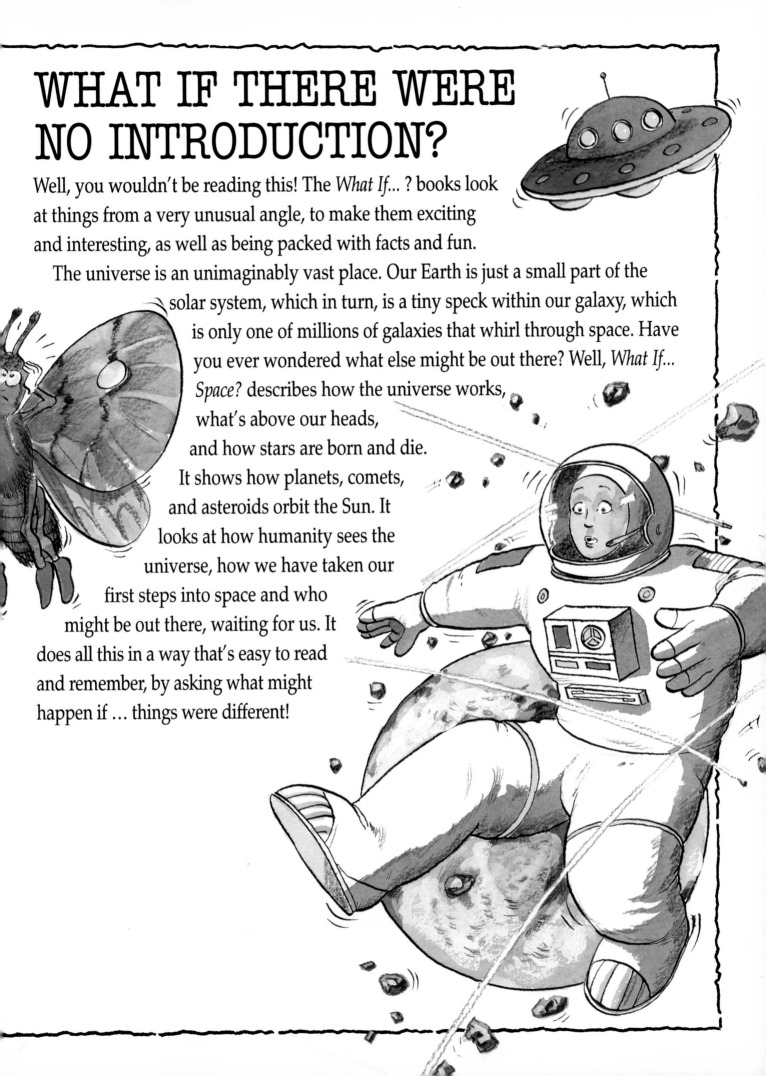

Well, you wouldn't be reading this! The *What If...?* books look at things from a very unusual angle, to make them exciting and interesting, as well as being packed with facts and fun.

The universe is an unimaginably vast place. Our Earth is just a small part of the solar system, which in turn, is a tiny speck within our galaxy, which is only one of millions of galaxies that whirl through space. Have you ever wondered what else might be out there? Well, *What If... Space?* describes how the universe works, what's above our heads, and how stars are born and die. It shows how planets, comets, and asteroids orbit the Sun. It looks at how humanity sees the universe, how we have taken our first steps into space and who might be out there, waiting for us. It does all this in a way that's easy to read and remember, by asking what might happen if … things were different!

WHAT IF THE TELESCOPE HADN'T BEEN INVENTED?

We would know very little about outer space, where stars, planets, moons, comets, and other objects hurtle at incredible speeds across unimaginably vast distances. Our knowledge about space was given a great boost by the Italian astronomer Galileo Galilei. In 1609 he turned a new-fangled telescope heavenward and saw the Moon and planets magnified. It was a new era in astronomy, the study of space, stars, and other heavenly objects. People have been star-gazing with telescopes ever since.

Geocentric or heliocentric?

In olden days, people believed in a geocentric system where the Sun, and all the planets orbited the Earth. However, astronomers such as Galileo, found that their observations did not match this theory. They proposed a heliocentric system, where the Earth orbits the Sun. Today, we know this system was correct.

Galileo's improved telescope made objects look much larger. He saw that our Moon has mountains and craters, and that Jupiter has its own moons.

How could we see galaxies?

Even without a telescope, you can see a galaxy. The faint streak across the night sky is called the *Milky Way*, which is made up of millions of stars. It's actually our own galaxy. Telescopes reveal millions of other galaxies, or clusters of stars, in space.

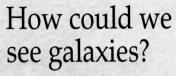

Why did an eclipse cause fear and terror?

Until people realized what happens during a solar eclipse (see page 11), these events caused panic and alarm. Many thought that angry gods were destroying the world, or that a massive dragon was trying to eat the Sun!

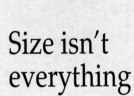

Size isn't everything

The universe is everything, including the Earth, the planets, the Sun, the stars, and space. Without telescopes, we couldn't see very far across the universe. With telescopes, we can detect incredibly distant objects. Scientists use these instruments to measure not only how large the universe is, but also how long it has been around.

What if telescopes worked without light?

They do. Light rays are just one tiny part of a whole range of rays called the *electromagnetic spectrum*. Stars send out light and other rays, such as X rays and gamma rays, into the spectrum. Radio telescopes with large dishes or long aerial wires and satellites detect the rays, to give us yet more information about space.

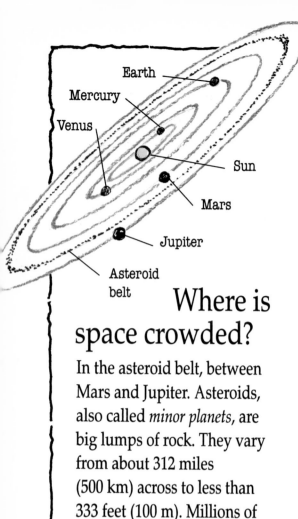

Earth
Mercury
Venus
Sun
Mars
Jupiter
Asteroid belt

WHAT IF SPACE WEREN'T SPACE?

The space between stars, planets, and other objects is not a complete vacuum (totally empty). There's a lot of emptiness, but there are rays and waves such as heat, light, radio waves, and X rays. There's also the odd molecule of hydrogen and other substances, sometimes forming huge clouds, called nebulae, that may be billions of miles across. There are also tiny particles, bits of dust, and pieces of rock called micrometeors, whizzing around. Near the Earth there's debris such as old rockets and satellites, space-station refuse, lost tools, and other waste. They all make spacewalks rather risky!

Where is space crowded?

In the asteroid belt, between Mars and Jupiter. Asteroids, also called *minor planets*, are big lumps of rock. They vary from about 312 miles (500 km) across to less than 333 feet (100 m). Millions of them make traveling through the asteroid belt very tricky!

What's a shooting star?

A famous movie actor with a gun? No, a shooting star is a lump of rock, called a meteor, that rushes through space and travels close to Earth. As it enters our atmosphere and pushes through the air, the friction, or rubbing, against the air molecules, makes it hot. The meteor glows redhot and burns up, creating a flash, or trail of light, known as a shooting star (falling star). A large meteor might not burn up completely, and can crash onto the Earth's surface as a meteorite.

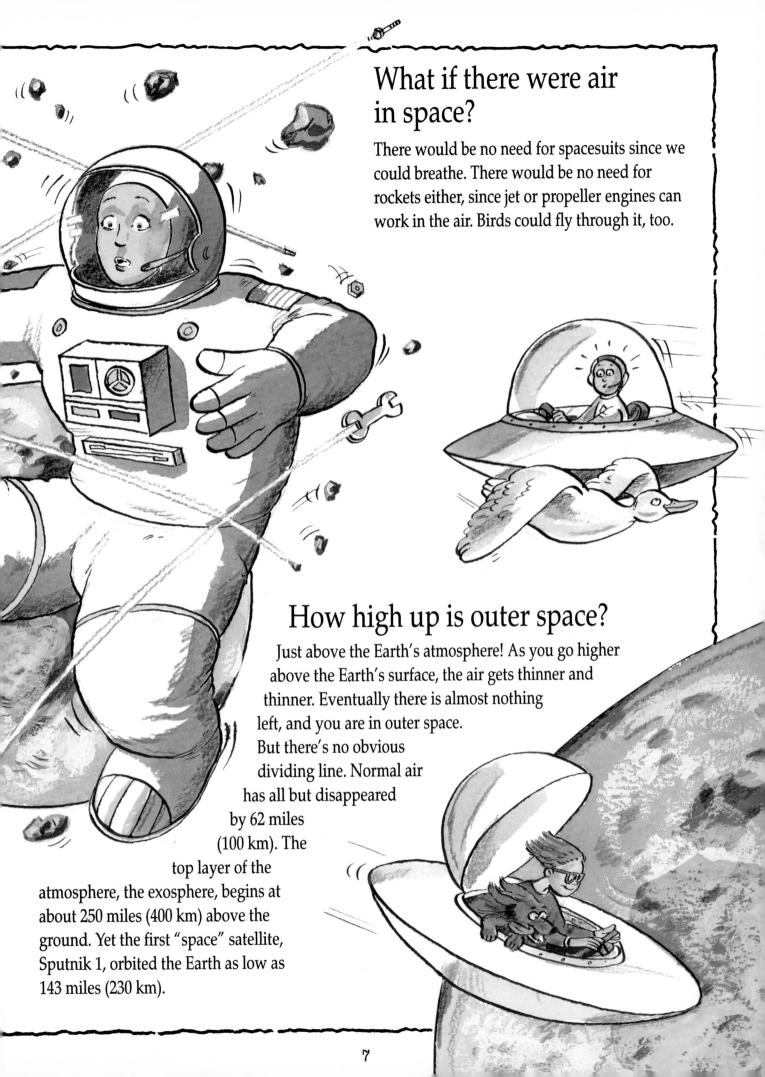

What if there were air in space?

There would be no need for spacesuits since we could breathe. There would be no need for rockets either, since jet or propeller engines can work in the air. Birds could fly through it, too.

How high up is outer space?

Just above the Earth's atmosphere! As you go higher above the Earth's surface, the air gets thinner and thinner. Eventually there is almost nothing left, and you are in outer space. But there's no obvious dividing line. Normal air has all but disappeared by 62 miles (100 km). The top layer of the atmosphere, the exosphere, begins at about 250 miles (400 km) above the ground. Yet the first "space" satellite, Sputnik 1, orbited the Earth as low as 143 miles (230 km).

7

Could we land on Venus?

Venus is similar in size to the Earth. But its atmosphere has clouds of corrosive sulfuric acid, and the surface temperature is 869°F (465°C). Not the place for a vacation!

Which planet is not named after a god?

All of the planets are named after Roman or Greek gods, except for Earth. It is named after the Old English word, "eorthe," meaning land or soil.

WHAT IF A SPACE PROBE TRIED TO LAND ON SATURN?

It would be very difficult, because there is hardly any "land" to land on! Saturn is the second largest planet, 75,335 miles (120,536 km) across, made up of mainly hydrogen and helium. A space probe would pass the planet's beautiful rings and disappear into the immense gas clouds of the atmosphere. As the probe fell deeper, the pressure would increase, and before long crush the probe. Further down, the pressure is so great that the gases are squeezed into liquid. The planet's core is a small, rocky lump.

The planet of fire and ice

Mercury, the planet closest to the Sun, is only 3,048 miles (4,878 km) in diameter. Its atmosphere has been blasted away by powerful solar winds. This rocky ball has daytime temperatures ranging from over 806°F (430°C) – hot enough to melt lead – to a bone-chilling -292°F (-180°C)!

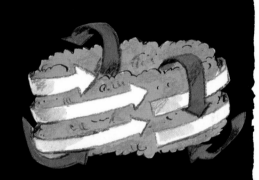

Stormy weather

Jupiter has a storm three times the size of Earth, about 25,000 miles (40,000 km) across. It's called the Great Red Spot, and drifts around the planet's lower half. A gigantic vortex sucks up corrosive phosphorus and sulfur, in a huge swirling spiral. At the top of this spiral, the chemicals spill out, forming the huge spot, before falling back into the planet's atmosphere.

Are there canals on Mars?

Not really. But there are channels or canyons. In 1877 Italian astronomer Giovanni Schiaparelli described lines crisscrossing the surface of the "Red Planet." He called them canali which means "channels."

What are planetary rings made of?

Saturn has the biggest and best rings – six main ones, made up of hundreds of ringlets. They are 175,000 miles (280,000 km) in diameter – twice the planet's width. They are made from blocks of rocks, ranging from a few inches to about 16 feet (5 m), swirling around the planet, and covered with glistening ice. Jupiter, Neptune, and Uranus also have fine rings.

Which planet is farthest from the Sun?

Pluto. No, Neptune. No – both! On average, Pluto is the outermost planet. This small, cold world is only 1,438 miles (2,300 km) across, with a temperature of -364°F (-220°C). Its orbit is squashed, so for some of the time, it's closer to the Sun than its neighbor Neptune. In fact, Pluto is within Neptune's orbit until 1999.

WHAT IF WE HAD MANY MOONS?

If the Earth had a lot of moons, night creatures might get confused. Moths use the Moon to find their way around – which would they choose if there were more than one? Owls, bats, and other night creatures might not wake up, as reflected light from the many Moons would keep the night sky bright. The Earth would also be more like the other planets. Most planets have lots of moons going around them. We have only one, which we call the Moon. At 2,160 miles (3,476 km) in diameter, it's much larger than most moons of other planets. With all these new moons we'd have to invent new names for them.

Is there a man in the moon?

No, but there were men on the Moon – the Apollo astronauts between 1969-1972. The patterns that we see on the Moon's surface, which resemble a crooked face, are made of giant mountains and massive craters. The craters, which can be as large as 625 miles (1,000 km) across, were made when asteroids and meteorites crashed into the Moon's surface.

The birth of a moon

Some scientists believe the Moon was probably formed at the same time as the Earth, from rocks whirling in space. Others think it was made when a planet crashed into the Earth, throwing up masses of debris, which clumped together to form the Moon. The moons of other planets may have been asteroids captured by the planet's gravity.

Which planet has the most moons?

At the moment Saturn has the most, with 18 moons as well as its colorful rings. This is followed by Jupiter with 16, and then Uranus which has 15. However, as telescopes get bigger and better, more moons may be discovered, so these numbers may change.

What happens if the Moon goes in front of the Sun?

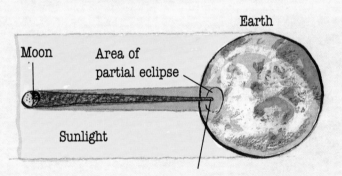

Moon

Area of partial eclipse

Earth

Sunlight

Area of total eclipse

It blocks out the Sun and casts a shadow on Earth, and we get a solar eclipse. But this does not happen all over the world. The total eclipse, with all the Sun hidden, is only in a small area. Around this is the area of partial eclipse, where the Sun appears to be only partly covered.

What's on the far side of the Moon?

The Moon goes around the Earth once every 27 days 8 hours. It also takes 27 days 8 hours to spin on its own axis. So the Moon always shows the same side to us. The far side of the Moon was first seen by the spacecraft Luna 3 in 1959, which sent back photographs of a lifeless moon, with no partying aliens!

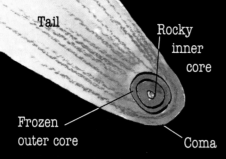

Tail

Rocky inner core

Frozen outer core

Coma

Inside a comet
A typical comet has a small center, or core, a few miles across. It's made from pieces of grit, dust, and crystals of frozen gases such as methane, ammonia, carbon dioxide, and water (ice).

WHAT IF COMETS DIDN'T RETURN?

Ancient civilizations thought a comet was a god breathing into the heavens or sending a fireball to destroy the Earth. At regular intervals they would streak across the night sky, creating fear and panic in all who saw them. Comets are really just lumps of ice and rock that boil and fizz as they near the Sun, sending out a huge tail of dust and vapor. In the 1700s it was noticed

that some comets kept returning, orbiting the Sun in a stretched-out circle, called a *parabola*. Some just disappear into deep space.

Crash, bang, smash

If a comet hit a planet, there would be a massive explosion. This was seen when the comet Shoemaker-Levy 9 collided with Jupiter in 1994. A series of explosions punched huge holes in the atmosphere, stirring up gases from Jupiter's interior.

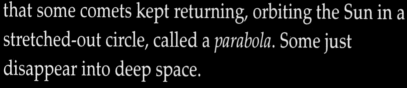

How do we know comets will return?

The British astronomer Edmond Halley noticed that the paths of comets observed in 1531 and 1607, and the one he saw in 1682, were all the same – was it the same comet returning each time? He predicted it would return in 1758. It did, and has since been called Halley's comet. From his theories, astronomers were able to plot comets' long orbits around the Sun.

How do we know what's inside a comet?

From observing its orbit and how fast it travels, by studying the light and other waves it gives out, and with space probes and telescopes. In 1986, five space probes passed near Halley's comet, on its regular visit. Europe's Giotto got within 375 miles (600 km) of the core, which is only 10 miles (16 km) long and 5 miles (8 km) wide, and sent back many photographs.

What if a comet didn't have a tail?

For much of its lifetime, it doesn't. As a comet travels close to the Sun and warms, its icy crust boils, throwing out gases that make a glowing outer layer, called the *coma*. The solar wind blows dust and other particles from the coma to form a tail that reflects the Sun's glow, and points away from the Sun. Then the comet heads into space, and the tail disappears.

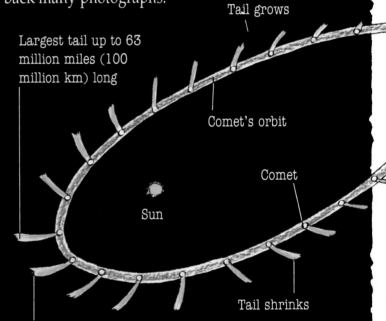

Tail grows

Largest tail up to 63 million miles (100 million km) long

Comet's orbit

Comet

Sun

Tail shrinks

Tail points away from Sun

How long do comets last?

Some fall to pieces after a few hundred years, while others may last millions of years. It depends partly on how often the comet travels near the Sun. Halley's comet has been seen every 75-76 years for over 2,000 years!

WHAT IF THE SUN WENT OUT?

Who turned off the lights? Why is it suddenly so cold? If the Sun no longer bathed our world in light and warmth, we might last a short time with fires, electric light, and oil or gas heat. But plants could not grow in the dark, and animals would perish from the cold. Soon all life would cease, and our planet would be dark and frozen. In fact this will happen, but not for billions of years. Our Sun is a fairly typical star, and stars do not last forever. They form, grow old, and either fade away or explode in a supernova, a massive explosion.

From the cradle to the grave

Throughout the universe there are massive clouds of gas, called *nebulae*. In some of these, the dust and particles clump together, and over millions of years, these clumps will form stars. Other nebulae are the wispy remains of a *supernova*, a star that has exploded.

What is a red giant?

An enormous human with red clothes? No, it is a star that has been growing and shining for billions of years, and is nearing the end of its life. As it ages, the star swells and its light turns red. Our Sun will do this in millions of years. It will expand to the size of a Red Giant, scorching our planet, before it explodes. Then all that will be left is a tiny white dwarf star that will slowly fade over millions of years.

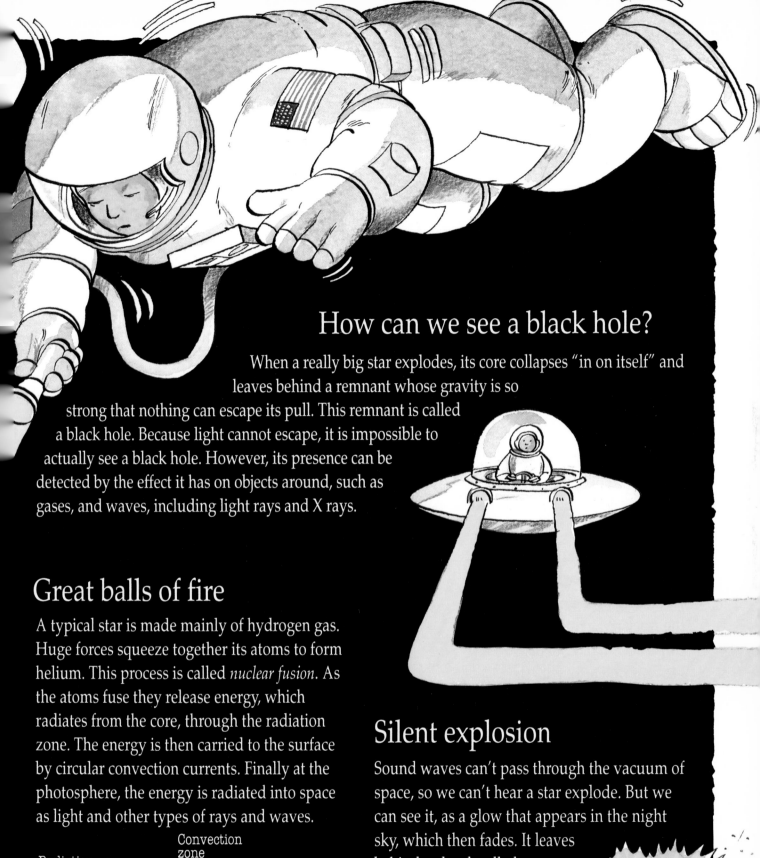

How can we see a black hole?

When a really big star explodes, its core collapses "in on itself" and leaves behind a remnant whose gravity is so strong that nothing can escape its pull. This remnant is called a black hole. Because light cannot escape, it is impossible to actually see a black hole. However, its presence can be detected by the effect it has on objects around, such as gases, and waves, including light rays and X rays.

Great balls of fire

A typical star is made mainly of hydrogen gas. Huge forces squeeze together its atoms to form helium. This process is called *nuclear fusion*. As the atoms fuse they release energy, which radiates from the core, through the radiation zone. The energy is then carried to the surface by circular convection currents. Finally at the photosphere, the energy is radiated into space as light and other types of rays and waves.

Silent explosion

Sound waves can't pass through the vacuum of space, so we can't hear a star explode. But we can see it, as a glow that appears in the night sky, which then fades. It leaves behind a cloud, called a *nebula*.

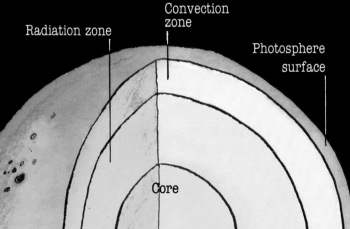

Radiation zone

Convection zone

Photosphere surface

Core

Dizzy galaxies

A galaxy is a group of billions of stars. Our own galaxy is called a spiral because it spins like a pinwheel. Other types of galaxies are ellipticals (oval) or irregulars (no shape). There are many other spiral galaxies like our own.

How did ancient civilizations view the universe?

Many ancient cultures were fascinated by the stars. According to some theories, the Ancient Egyptians tried to construct a replica of the heavens on Earth, with the Nile representing the Milky Way, and the three great pyramids as Orion's belt.

WHAT IF THERE WERE NO STARS AT NIGHT?

Sometimes there aren't, if it's cloudy. Well, the stars are still there, but we can't see them. Without stars, the ancient Greeks and others wouldn't have spent hours gazing at them. They could see the outlines of people, animals, and objects in the star patterns. The constellations, which include Orion (the Hunter), Scorpio (the Scorpion), and Centaur (half man, half horse), are based on figures from Greek myths. Navigators couldn't have found their way across the seas and oceans without using the stars.

Zoo in the sky

The stars in the night sky are divided into patterns and groups, known as *constellations* (see above). These were named after people from legends, objects, and even animals. The northern hemisphere has two bears: The Great Bear (Ursa major), and The Little Bear (Ursa minor). Find some star charts and try to look for them tonight. The night sky also has a bird of paradise (Apus), an eagle (Aquila), a ram (Aries), a toucan (Tucana), a wolf (Lupus), two dogs (Canis major and Canis minor), a whale (Cetus), and a snake (Serpens).

What if the stars moved?

They do. Stars in our spiral galaxy are spinning around. Our Sun takes over 200 million years to orbit the center of the galaxy. As the stars move, star patterns and constellations gradually change. In thousands of years, constellations will be different, and today's star charts will be out-of-date.

What if planets shone, like stars?

It would probably never get dark! Planets shine, but only because they reflect the light from the Sun. However, they are not massive enough to start the process of nuclear fusion which makes stars shine (see page 15).

WHAT IF THE UNIVERSE STARTED TO SHRINK?

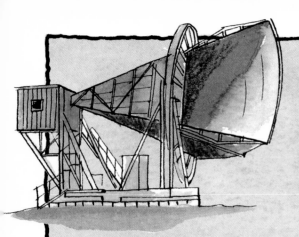

Most experts believe that the universe began as a tiny speck containing all matter, which blew up billions of years ago in a massive explosion, called the Big Bang. It's been getting bigger ever since, as galaxies fly away from one another. This may go on forever, or the universe might reach a certain size, and then maintain a steady state, or it could begin to shrink. All the planets, stars, galaxies, and other matter might squeeze back together to form a tiny speck as the opposite of the Big Bang – the Big Crunch.

What was the Big Bang?

It was the beginning of the universe: the time when all matter began to explode and expand, from a small core full of incredible heat, light, and energy. Was there anything before the Big Bang, like a supreme being? No one knows. There may have been no "before." Space, matter, energy, and even time may have started with the Big Bang.

Strings and clusters

Our galaxy is only one of millions found throughout the universe. Together with a few others, such as the Andromeda galaxy, it forms the *Local Group*, a collection, or cluster of galaxies that circle around space together. The Local Group is, in turn, part of a group of galaxy clusters known as a *supercluster*. These superclusters are linked by massive strings of galaxies that may be up to 300 million light-years long.

How far can we look across our universe?

As telescopes become more powerful, and orbit in space on satellites, they can pick up the faint light and other waves from more distant stars and galaxies. The farthest object currently visible is Quasar (QUASi-stellAR object) 4C41.17. This object is so far away that light reaching us now left the galaxy when the universe was one-fifth its current age.

Happy birthday to you...

The general agreement is that the universe was "born" in the Big Bang about 14 billion years ago. Some believe that it is closer to 17 billion or as low as 10 billion years old. Scientists are still arguing about its exact age. You would need a very big cake for all the birthday candles!

WHAT IF THERE WERE NO SPACECRAFT?

How would astronauts get back to Earth?

An astronaut could survive in a spacesuit for a short time. But coming back into Earth's atmosphere creates lots of heat, as an object pushes through the ever-thickening air molecules. A heat shield might help a rear-first re-entry!

Space exploration would be much less exciting without spacecraft that carry people. It began with the Space Race in the 1950s and 1960s. The United States and Russia raced to launch the first satellite, the first spaceman and woman, and the first Moon visit. The satellite Sputnik 1, launched in 1957, was the first man-made object in space, and the Russian Yuri Gagarin was the first man in space. But the United States was first to land on the Moon in 1969 with the spacecraft Apollo 11 carrying Neil Armstrong and Edwin "Buzz" Aldrin. Without spacecraft, none of these achievements would have happened.

What would Yuri Gagarin have done?

Yuri was the very first person in space. On April 12, 1961, he orbited Earth once in his ball-shaped spacecraft Vostok 1. Without this spacecraft, he would never have become world famous. But he could have carried on as a successful test pilot for the Russian Air Force.

What if there were no satellites?

We would have no satellite TV or satellite weather pictures, and mobile phones would not work very well. Ships, planes, and overland explorers could not use their satellite navigation gadgets. Without satellites, countries would have to find new ways to spy on each other. They could go back to the high-flying spyplanes used just after World War II, or use high-flying balloons carrying surveillance equipment.

How much money would we save?

Space programs run throughout the world by different countries, like the Apollo Moon missions, have cost billions of dollars. Manned space flights are the most expensive type of missions. It has been estimated that NASA has spent over $80 billion on its manned space flights up to 1994, with nearly $45 billion spent on the space shuttle program alone! Even a single spacesuit worn outside the space shuttle costs $3.4 million!

Nonstick earthlings

Our everyday lives have been affected by the enormous technological leaps made during the age of space exploration. These "leaps" include nonstick coatings, used for lubrication in spacecraft. Also, the microtechnology needed in satellites has led to smaller and faster computers, some found in household appliances.

WELCOME EARTHLINGS!

WHAT IF ROCKETS HADN'T BEEN INVENTED?

We would still be wondering about the empty space above us, instead of launching astronauts into space and sending probes on space missions. A rocket can fly fast enough to get into space. To do this, it must reach the speed called *escape velocity*, 17,700 mph (28,500 km/h), to escape from the pull of Earth's gravity. A rocket engine can work in airless space, unlike jets and other engines, as explained below. The other way to get into space might be a gigantic gun that fires spacecraft and satellites into space. However, any astronaut would be crushed by the g-forces of acceleration!

Dawn of the rocket age

The first rockets used a type of gunpowder and flew in warfare in China, in A.D. 1232. The first modern rocket to use the liquid fuel that today's rockets use was launched by American scientist Robert Goddard in 1926.

Why can't jets fly in space?

Like a jet engine, a rocket burns fuel in a type of continuous explosion. Hot gases blast out of the back, and thrust the engine forward. Space has no air, which is needed for the burning that takes place inside the jet engine. A rocket must carry its own supply of oxygen.

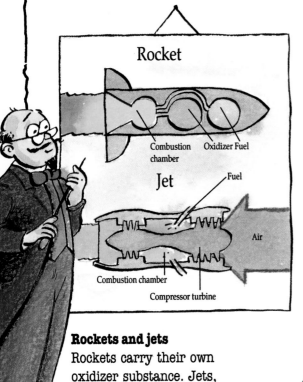

Rocket

Combustion chamber   Oxidizer Fuel

Jet   Fuel

Air

Combustion chamber

Compressor turbine

Rockets and jets
Rockets carry their own oxidizer substance. Jets, however, need oxygen from the air to burn their fuel.

Up, up, and away in my beautiful balloon

Special weather balloons go higher than 31 miles (50 km). They carry radiosondes that measure temperature, air pressure, and humidity, and send back the results by radio. The balloon is quite small and floppy when it takes off, but it gradually expands as it rises, as the air pressure decreases. However, no weather balloon could carry a heavy satellite high enough, or give it the required speed to put it in orbit.

Would we have fabulous firework displays?

Perhaps, but we would have to power the rockets by other types of engines, maybe a mini jet engine. Firework rockets use solid fuel such as gunpowder or other fuel-oxidizer mixtures to launch into the air. Many space rockets use liquid fuel, and have the propellant and oxidizer in liquid form.

Multi-staged rockets

A staged rocket may have two, three, or more rockets, placed on top of each other in decreasing size. The biggest one launches the entire rocket, then stops firing and falls away. The rocket's weight is now less and so is the effect of the Earth's gravity, so the second-stage rocket is much smaller, and so on with the remaining stages. Extra rockets, called boosters, may assist the main rocket engine at launch and then fall away, as in the space shuttle.

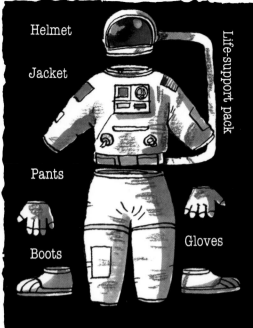

Helmet

Jacket

Pants

Boots

Gloves

Life-support pack

Sections of a spacesuit
The suit has various parts, and it takes a long time to put on. All the joints must be airtight, to maintain proper air pressure and temperature.

WHAT IF THE SPACESUIT HADN'T BEEN INVENTED?

Astronauts are safe in space, if they stay inside their spacecraft. Outside, there is no air to breathe, and it is incredibly cold (or hot). There are lots of dangerous rays and radiations, and micrometeors travel as fast as tiny bullets. The space suit is shiny to reflect rays of radiation. It contains its own *life-support systems* that control the air and temperature. It also has special layers to protect against impact from debris. In space, any other type of suit, like a deep-sea diver's suit, would be no good at all!

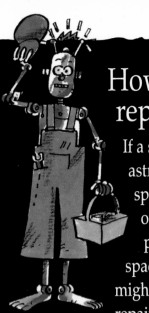

How could we repair satellites?

If a satellite malfunctions, astronauts can maneuver their spacecraft near it, then float over in a spacesuit with a jet-pack, to make repairs. If spacesuits didn't exist we might have to invent a robot repairman!

Would Alexei Leonov be so famous?

This Russian astronaut became famous on March 18, 1965. He was first to use a spacesuit to leave his spacecraft for a space "walk," floating weightlessly, miles above the Earth.

Could people have landed on the Moon?

Yes, but they wouldn't have been able to walk around. The bootprints of the Apollo astronauts will be in the dust for thousands of years.

Leaky spacesuits

The suit contains a mixture of gases for breathing. It's under pressure, to simulate the Earth's atmosphere. If it squirts away through a leak, the astronaut will be in great danger!

What if spacesuits weren't cooled?

Or warmed, either? In Earth's orbit, the astronaut orbits the planet in about 90 minutes. He would get boiling hot while in the glare of the Sun. As he circled around to the night side, he'd freeze to death! The spacesuit keeps his body temperature within a more comfortable range.

NEAREST STAR 237,000,000,000,000 MILES

WHAT IF WE COULD TRAVEL AT THE SPEED OF LIGHT?

Almost everything in the universe varies from place to place, such as temperature, pressure, gravity, and the size and mass of objects. However, the speed of light is always the same – 186,282 miles per second (299,792 kilometers per second). As you approach the speed of light, strange things happen, according to Albert Einstein's theory of relativity.

What is a light-year?

Is it 365 sunny days? No, it is not a measure of time, but of distance. It's the distance that light travels in one year. Since light travels very fast, a light-year is extremely far – about 5.88 trillion miles (9.46 trillion km) Even so, space is so vast that a light-year is a tiny distance.

Time slows down, and objects get smaller and heavier. Modern science says that no physical matter could travel faster than light, or even at the speed of light. However, radio waves and X rays travel as fast as light, since they are part of the same electromagnetic spectrum.

Space, the final frontier...

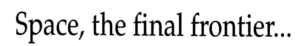

In science fiction stories, such as *Star Trek*, characters are always traveling from solar system to solar system in search of adventure. However, even if we could travel at the speed of light, it would still take over four years to reach Proxima Centauri, our nearest star after the Sun. Even then, we would have to find a planet to land on.

NCC-1701

Could we reach the nearest galaxy?

Not unless science came up with some amazing new theories about travel and going faster than the speed of light. The closest galaxy to our own is the Large Magellanic Cloud (LMC), only 17,000 light-years from home! Other nearby galaxies are the Small Magellanic Cloud (SMC), M31 Andromeda, M32, and M33 Triangulum Spiral. Together they form part of the Local Group of galaxies, in our part of the universe. If we tried to go to another galaxy in a spacecraft like the shuttle, it would take millions of years.

How long would it take to get to a planet?

Mars is probably the best example. It's quite close – it's the nearest planet and also has hard ground to land on, as the Vikings showed (see page 28). With current spacecraft technology, the journey might take 10 months. With the ground mission, the whole trip would last two years.

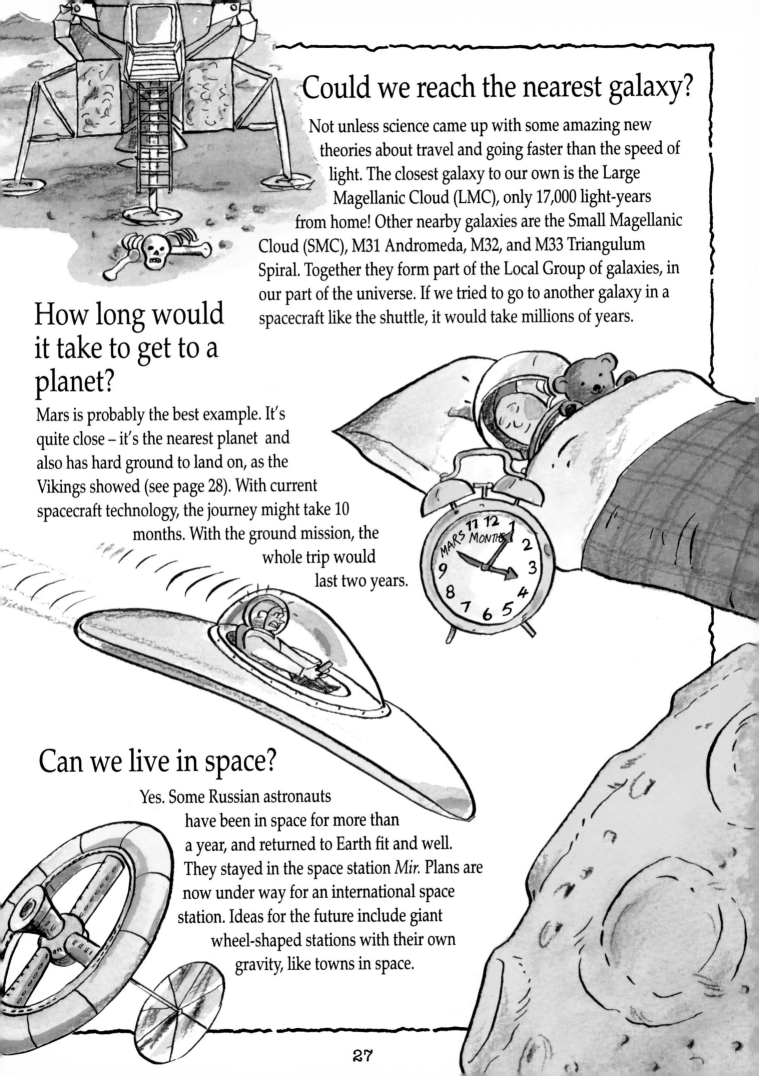

Can we live in space?

Yes. Some Russian astronauts have been in space for more than a year, and returned to Earth fit and well. They stayed in the space station *Mir*. Plans are now under way for an international space station. Ideas for the future include giant wheel-shaped stations with their own gravity, like towns in space.

WHAT IF THERE WERE MARTIANS?

Are UFOs real?

Unidentified Flying Objects certainly do exist. People, including jet-plane pilots, see things in the sky they cannot identify. But are they alien spacecraft? They could be test planes, meteors, or even the planet Venus!

The space probes, Vikings 1 and 2, landed on Mars in 1976. They found a reddish, dusty, rock-strewn landscape. But their cameras, sensors, and experiments detected no proper sign of life. In August 1993, as the space probe Mars Observer approached its destination, its radio failed, and all went silent. Was it sabotaged by shy, secretive Martians? Probably not. Scientists estimate that among 10 billion galaxies, there are trillions of stars, and probably some that have planets like Earth – maybe these have some kind of life.

Are aliens trying to get in touch with us?

Perhaps, but messages in bottles won't work! Only light, radio, and similar waves travel through space at great speed. Aliens might send messages as coded patterns of waves. Radio telescopes used for the National Aeronautics and Space Administration's (NASA) Search for ExtraTerrestrial Intelligence project (SETI) have failed to detect such waves.

Are we trying to send messages to aliens?

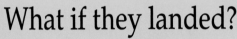

Yes, we send bursts of radio messages into space. Also, space probes carry messages in case they are found by aliens. Space probes such as Pioneers 10 and 11 have plaques with drawings of humans, and a star map showing where we are.

What if they landed?

There's a plan for dealing with aliens, but it's top secret. Anyway, aliens advanced enough for space travel would be much smarter than we are. So it might not matter what we did. We just hope they are friendly!

Evidence of alien landings

A few strange cave drawings, paintings, sculptures, and rock patterns from ancient times, might suggest that aliens visited Earth long ago. Some people say that over the years, aliens have helped us. But there's no real proof, and that's what scientists require.

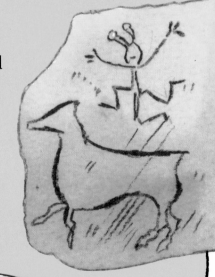

FACTFILE

PLANET PROFILES

Planetary year is time taken to make one orbit of the Sun
Planetary day is time taken to spin once on axis

MERCURY
Diameter: 3,031 miles (4,878 km)
Average distance from Sun:
  36 million miles (58 million km)
Planetary year: 88 Earth days
Planetary day: 59 Earth days
Surface temperature range:
  –292 to 806 °F (–183°C to 430°C)

VENUS
Diameter: 7,520 miles (12,105 km)
Average distance from Sun:
  67 million miles (108 million km)
Planetary year: 225 Earth days
Planetary day: 243 Earth days
Surface temperature:
  av. 869°F (465°C)

EARTH
Diameter: 7,926 miles (12,756 km)
Average distance from Sun:
  93 million miles (150 million km)
Planetary year: 365 days
Planetary day: 24 hours
Surface temperature:
  av. 59°F (15°C)

MARS
Diameter: 4,217 miles (6,786 km)
Average distance from Sun:
  142 million miles (228 million km)
Planetary year: 687 Earth days
Planetary day: 24.6 Earth hours
Surface temperature range:
  –207 to 72°F (–133 to 22°C)

JUPITER
Diameter: 88,846 miles
  (142,984 km)
Average distance from Sun:
  483 million miles
  (778 million km)
Planetary year: 11.8 Earth years
Planetary day: 9.9 Earth hours
Surface temperature:
  av. –238°F (–150°C)

SATURN
Diameter: 74,898 miles
  (120,536 km)
Average distance from Sun:
  887 million miles
  (1,427 million km)
Planetary year: 29.5 Earth years
Planetary day: 10.5 Earth hours
Surface temperature:
  av. –292°F (–180°C)

URANUS
Diameter: 31,763 miles (51,118 km)
Average distance from Sun:
  1,784 million miles
  (2,871 million km)
Planetary year: 84 Earth years
Planetary day: 17.25 Earth hours
Surface temperature:
  av. –346°F (–210°C)

NEPTUNE
Diameter: 30,775 miles (49,528 km)
Average distance from Sun:
  2,794 million miles
  (4,497 million km)
Planetary year: 164.8 Earth years
Planetary day: 16 Earth hours
Surface temperature:
  av. –346°F (–210°C)

PLUTO
Diameter: 1,419 miles (2,280 km)
Average distance from Sun:
  3,688 million miles
  (5,900 million km)
Planetary year: 247.7 Earth years
Planetary day: 6.4 Earth days
Surface temperature:
  av. –364°F (–220°C)

Neptune   Saturn   Mars   Venus   Earth   Pluto

Sun   Mercury   Jupiter   Uranus

The Solar System

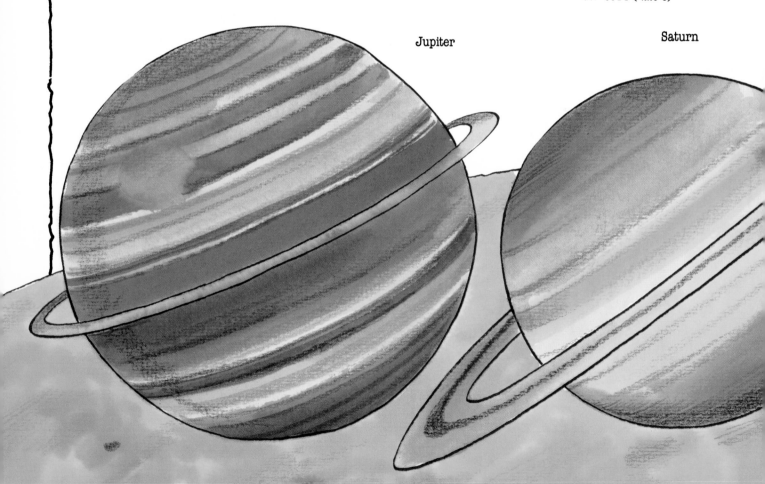

Jupiter

Saturn

GLOSSARY

FROM BIG TO SMALL

Universe Everything, including all galaxies, stars, planets, and other objects, as well as the space, cosmic dust, and all other matter between them.

Galaxy A huge group or cluster of stars relatively close together, separated from other galaxies by vast empty space. Our own galaxy is called the Galaxy or Milky Way.

Quasar (Quasi-stellar object) A mysterious and extremely distant object that shines like many galaxies, but which seems smaller in size than one galaxy. It may be a galaxy being born.

Solar system A group of planets that orbit a star. Our solar system has a total of nine planets that go around the Sun.

Star In astronomy, a star is an object that gives out energy as light, heat, and other forms of radiation. In other words, it shines under its own power.

Sun Our local star, which seems so bright and warm because it's relatively close to us. The Sun is quite small, and is called a yellow dwarf.

White dwarf A small type or stage in the life of a star, possibly not much bigger than a planet such as Jupiter. It is usually a star that is reaching the end of its life.

Planet A relatively large object that goes around a star, such as the nine planets orbiting the Sun.

Moon An object in space that orbits (goes around) a larger object, usually a planet. Earth has one large moon, which we call the *Moon*. Moons are also satellites.

Asteroid A small, rocky body that is also known as a minor planet. In our solar system the greatest concentration of asteroids is in the asteroid belt between the planets Mars and Jupiter.

Satellite An object in space that orbits (goes around) a larger object. So Earth is a satellite of the Sun, and the Moon is a satellite of the Earth. But the word "satellite" is usually used to mean an artificial or man-made space object.

Black hole A region in space that has incredible gravity, so nothing can escape from it, not even light or other forms of energy. Any nearby matter is pulled into it.

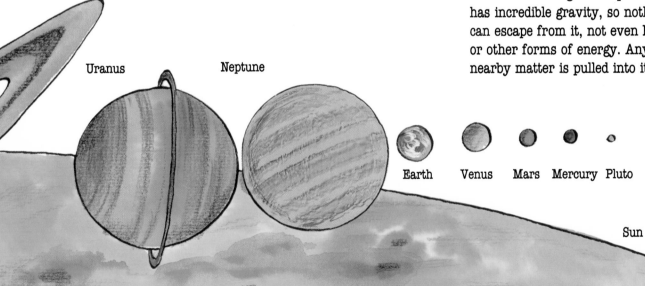

Uranus Neptune Earth Venus Mars Mercury Pluto Sun

INDEX

alien 11, 28, 29
Apollo 10
asteroid 10, 31
asteroid belt 6, 10
astronaut 20, 22, 24, 25, 27
astronomy 4

Big Bang 18
black hole 15, 31

Centaur 16
comet 4, 12, 13
  comet, Halley's 13

Earth 4, 6, 7, 8, 9, 10, 11, 13, 20, 22, 30, 31
eclipse 5, 11
escape velocity 22

Gagarin, Yuri 20
galaxy 5, 16, 18, 19, 27, 28, 31
  Andromeda 19, 27
  elliptical 16
  irregular 16
  Local Group 19, 27
  spiral 16, 17
Galileo Galilei 4
gamma rays 5
gases 8, 9, 12, 13, 14, 25
geocentric system 4
gravity 22, 27
Great Red Spot 9

Halley, Edmond 13
heliocentric system 4

Jupiter 4, 6, 9, 11, 12, 13, 30, 31

Leonov, Alexei 25
light rays 15
light-year 19, 26
luna 3, 11

Mars 6, 9, 27, 28, 30, 31
Martians 28, 29
Mercury 6, 9, 30, 31
meteor 6, 28
meteorite 6, 10
Milky Way 5, 16
Mir 27
Moon 4, 10-11, 20, 25, 31

NASA 21
nebula 15
nebulae 6, 14, 15
Neptune 9, 30, 31
nuclear fusion 15, 17

Orion's belt 16

planetary day 30
planetary year 30
planets 4, 6, 8, 9, 10, 12, 13, 18, 30, 31
Pluto 9, 30, 31

quasar 19, 31

radio telescopes 5, 18
radio wave 5, 6, 26
red giant 14
rocket 7, 22-23
  boosters 23
  multi-staged 23

satellite 5, 6, 7, 19, 21, 22, 23, 25, 31
Saturn 8, 9, 11, 13, 30, 31
solar system 4, 8-9, 26, 31
spacecraft 20-21

space probe 8-9, 13, 28, 29
Space Race 20
space shuttle 23
spacesuit 7, 24-25
Sputnik I 7, 20
star 4, 5, 6, 14, 15, 16-17, 18, 28, 31
  shooting star 6
  star map 29
Sun 4, 5, 6, 9, 11, 12, 13, 14, 17, 31
supercluster 19
supernova 14

telescope 4-5, 11, 13, 19, 29

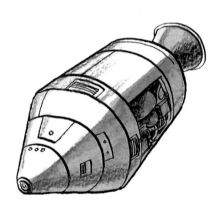

UFO 28
universe 5, 14, 18-19, 26, 27, 31

Venus 6, 8, 28, 30, 31
Vostok I 20

white dwarf 14, 31

X rays 5, 6, 15, 26

PRINTED IN BELGIUM BY
proost
INTERNATIONAL BOOK PRODUCTION